Contact Centers

FOR
DUMMIES®
AVAYA LIMITED EDITION

By Réal Bergevin and Allen Wyatt

WILEY

Wiley Publishing, Inc.

Contact Centers For Dummies, Avaya Limited Edition
Published by
Wiley Publishing, Inc.
111 River St.
Hoboken, NJ 07030-5774
www.wiley.com

Copyright © 2005 by Wiley Publishing, Inc., Indianapolis, Indiana

Published by Wiley Publishing, Inc., Indianapolis, Indiana

Published simultaneously in Canada

For general information on our other products and services, please contact our Customer Care Department within the U.S. at 800-762-2974, outside the U.S. at 317-572-3993, or fax 317-572-4002.

For technical support, please visit www.wiley.com/techsupport.

Wiley also publishes its books in a variety of electronic formats. Some content that appears in print may not be available in electronic books.

ISBN-13: 978-0-471-75819-8

ISBN-10: 0-471-75819-1

Manufactured in the United States of America

10 9 8 7 6 5 4 3 2

1O/SX/QX/QV/IN

WILEY

Publisher's Acknowledgments

We're proud of this book; please send us your comments through our Dummies online registration form located at www.dummies.com/register/. For information about a custom Dummies book for your company or organization, contact BrandedRights&Licenses@Wiley.com.

Some of the people who helped bring this book to market include the following:

Acquisitions, Editorial, and Media Development

Project Editor: Janet Withers

Business Development Representative: Jacqueline Smith

Branded Products Coordinator: Gabriele McCann

Editorial Manager: Rev Mengle

Composition Services

Project Coordinator: Kristie Rees

Layout and Graphics: Andrea Dahl, Stephanie D. Jumper, Heather Ryan

Proofreaders: Leeann Harney, Jessica Kramer

Special Help: Yvonne Ba, Cory Glover, Lisa Kluberspies, Kay Phelps, Win Ross

Publishing and Editorial for Consumer Dummies

> **Diane Graves Steele,** Vice President and Publisher, Consumer Dummies
>
> **Joyce Pepple,** Acquisitions Director, Consumer Dummies
>
> **Kristin A. Cocks,** Product Development Director, Consumer Dummies
>
> **Michael Spring,** Vice President and Publisher, Travel
>
> **Kelly Regan,** Editorial Director, Travel

Publishing for Technology Dummies

> **Andy Cummings,** Vice President and Publisher, Dummies Technology/General User

Composition Services

> **Gerry Fahey,** Vice President of Production Services
>
> **Debbie Stailey,** Director of Composition Services

Table of Contents

Introduction

● ●

*W*elcome to *Contact Centers For Dummies,* Avaya Limited Edition. Executives and analysts alike realize more than ever that the contact center can have a tremendous impact on their overall business in the areas of revenue, costs, market intelligence, and customer loyalty.

A contact center is many things — cost center, profit center, key source of revenue, key source of frustration, strategic weapon, strategic disadvantage, source of marketing research, source of marketing paralysis — all depending on the goals and capabilities of the contact center.

About This Book

With the emergence of worldwide competition in the contact center business, it's become increasingly important for contact center professionals to work from a defined methodology. This guide attempts to provide a high-level approach to the different methodologies you can use. Here you can find lots of information not only on running contact centers, but also on implementing technology in contact centers in a profitable way.

Incidentally, this book could equally well have been named *Call Centers For Dummies.* Many businesses refer to a contact center as a call center because its main function is to answer incoming phone calls. With emerging technologies blurring the line between phone, e-mail, and other forms of contact, the generic term "contact center" seems more appropriate than ever. Don't worry, though — if your operation is referred to as a call center, this book is still for you.

Why You Need This Book

Those involved in the contact center industry will find this book an easy-to-use, plain-English reference guide to the effective operation of contact centers. It can be of particular use to you if:

- You're a hot-shot MBA tracking through your career and you find yourself running a contact center.

- You're an experienced contact center manager and you're looking for some new ideas and perspectives.

- You're a supplier to the contact center industry and want to better understand your clients' management challenges.

- You're working in a contact center and want to advance your career by unlocking the ancient contact center secrets found in this book.

How This Book Is Organized

Contact Centers For Dummies is organized into seven parts, each covering a different aspect of contact centers from resource management to the latest technologies that can help you plan for the future of contact centers. Any approach you take to tackling *Contact Centers For Dummies* is fine. Most people, however, will get the most out of this book by jumping right into Part I.

In Part I, "Contact Centers: A First Look," you'll get a good overview of contact centers. It's especially useful for those who are just getting started or who want to refresh their understanding of contact center basics or of current trends in contact center management.

Part II, "Business Basics: Models and Drivers and Goals, Oh My!," is especially for those planning a new contact center. You'll find a potential business model for building a contact center and relate that model to the larger corporate mission and goals.

Next comes Part III, "The Master Plan: Finance, Analysis, and Resource Management." This part looks at contact center analysis, financial planning, and staffing. Included is a simple overview of how (and what) measures come together to drive contact center operational and financial performance.

Part IV, "Making It Go: An Introduction to Contact Center Technology," covers the basic contact center technologies. You'll discover the various ways of getting contacts to the center, information to the agents, and information to customers.

In Part V, "Technological Enhancements: Getting the Newest and Coolest Stuff," you get into the fun stuff. Here you find the latest and greatest technologies available for updating and improving your contact center, new or existing. (To help you garner support for your toy list, you'll also find a simple approach to recommending and justifying new technology.)

Part VI, "Ten Ways to Improve Your Contact Center," provides tips and techniques to boost your company's revenue and efficiency. All ten suggestions should apply to any contact center, regardless of the types of contacts you handle.

Finally, at the end of this book you can find a helpful case study about one company's experiences in establishing a contact center with state-of-the-art Avaya technology. You can undoubtedly find parallels in their challenges and experiences to your own!

Icons Used in This Book

These are real-world stories about companies that have found successful technological solutions to a broad range of contact center and network management scenarios from Avaya applications and routing systems.

This is unforgettable stuff — or at least, you don't want to forget it.

The Tip icon provides you with a general recommendation on how you can make your contact center better, or make running your contact center easier.

This icon designates insider techie information you probably don't need to know but may find interesting.

This icon flags potential pitfalls you need to be careful of.

Part I

Contact Centers: A First Look

• •

In This Chapter

▶ Defining a contact center

▶ Inbound, outbound, internal, and external designations

▶ Differentiating between good and bad contact centers

▶ A quick glimpse into the future

• •

*N*o company operates in a vacuum, devoid of contact with customers or the general public. If you have the need to communicate with others outside of your company (who doesn't?), then you are a prime candidate for developing or using a contact center. Heck, you may already have a contact center and not even know it!

This chapter introduces you to contact centers — what they are and how they benefit customers and companies. You'll even discover some of the traits that distinguish a good contact center from a bad one. By the end of the chapter you should have a good grasp of how good management, sound skills, and great technology can help make a good contact center into a great one.

What Is a Contact Center?

We've all seen it — an ad on TV urging you to call right away. It's late at night, and some disgustingly perky announcer is touting the benefit of the latest laser-sharpened steak knives, full-chicken roaster, or Patsy Cline collection. In a moment of weakness, you pick up the phone and feverishly dial the number on the screen. Within seconds, you are connected to someone willing to send you whatever it is that you can no longer live without.

The person on the other end of the phone (who also happens to be way too perky for your 2:00 a.m. call) is undoubtedly part of a contact center, waiting for your call and ready to help.

But wait — there's more! (Sorry; I almost felt perky for a moment.) Contact centers aren't limited to late-night calls to sales people. A contact center is the person at the other end of the phone when you call an airline, cable company, technical support, or even your local health spa.

Sometimes a contact center is just one or two people sitting beside a phone answering customer calls. Often it's a very large room with lots and lots of people neatly organized into rows, sitting beside their phones, answering customer calls.

But contact centers are more than headset-wearing switchboard operators. The modern contact center handles phone calls, e-mail, online communication, and sometimes even old-fashioned written letters. In short, contact centers deal with any type of contact for a company (other than in-person) — contact with the general public and customers of all types: potential, happy, or even disgruntled. Contact — good, bad, or downright ugly — is the name of the game.

To a customer or client, contact center personnel are the voice and face of the company. If you (as a customer) are angry, you often get mad at the person on the other end of the phone — after all, you're talking to the company, right?

Inbound/outbound

Contact centers communicate with customers in a number of ways, but who initiates the contact defines the type of contact center. If the outside world initiates contact, then the contact center is said to be an *inbound contact center*. Conversely, if the contact center itself is responsible for initiating contact, then the contact center is said to be an *outbound contact center.*

Customers contact inbound centers to buy things, such as airline tickets; to get technical assistance with their personal computer; to get answers to questions about their utility bill; to get emergency assistance when their car won't start; or for any number of other reasons for which they might need to talk to a company representative.

In outbound centers, representatives from the company initiate the call to customers. Your first reaction might be, "telemarketing, right?" Well, yes, telemarketing is a reason for a company to contact you, but companies have lots of other good reasons to contact their customers, as well.

Companies might call because the customer hasn't paid a bill, when a product the customer wanted is available, to follow up on a problem the customer was having, or to find out what the customer and other customers would like to see by way of product or service enhancements.

Outbound contact centers are, most often, very telephone-centric. Whereas inbound centers can handle many different ways of contact, outbound centers most often use telephones because of, well, tradition and perception. It is not unusual for a company's representatives to call a customer on the phone, but it is more unusual for them to send an e-mail to a customer. If companies send out e-mail to customers, it is often done through some mass-mailing effort, not as one-on-one contact. Perception enters into the picture because people are very quick to categorize unexpected e-mail as spam, but less likely to be upset by unexpected phone calls.

In addition, a new breed of inbound centers is starting to emerge — *self-service* centers. In traditional contact centers, all interaction between the customer and the center is done with human agents. However, in self-service centers a good portion of the load is being shifted toward non-human systems, such as automated response or even speech-enabled.

Automated response systems enable the customer to use the keypad on their phone to answer questions by pushing buttons. Each button push brings them closer to the information they want. Automated response systems have been around for years, giving the customer access to simple (and common) information, such as addresses, balances, and procedural instructions.

Speech-enabled systems are more sophisticated and easier for the customer to use. In such a system the customer actually speaks a response, rather than needing to press keypad buttons. Speech-enabled systems are a great boon for cell-phone using customers because they no longer need to perform gymnastics to keep pressing buttons on their phone. As speech-enabled systems become more sophisticated, customers will be able to ask questions directly to the self-service system and get a wide variety of answers.

Some contact centers are called *blended* operations — agents in the center handle both inbound and outbound contact. Blending done well can make contact center operations very cost-effective and can improve service to the customer as well.

Internal/external

Just as contact centers can be designed as inbound or outbound, they can also be designated as internal or external. (I almost said in-house or out-house, but figured that the unintended allusion might be distracting.)

When companies are small, they often develop their own contact center capabilities internally. As companies grow, they often look to outsource their contact center functions, or they spin off those functions to a subsidiary or partner company. This is where the concept of the external contact center comes into play — the center is *external* to the main company.

In fact, companies that provide nothing but contact center functions to other companies have grown into a multi-million-dollar industry. At last count the traditional call center industry employed more than 6 million people in North America alone, and accounted for the sale of more than $700 billion in goods and services. Through today's contact centers you can purchase, complain, or just talk about almost anything from the comfort of your home, office, car, or wherever you can get to a phone (or log on to the Internet).

Whether your contact center consists of a receptionist and a customer service person or entire departments, the principles by which a contact center are operated are still the same. People involved in customer contact need the same skills and the same tools, regardless of the number of people involved. Thus, the information in this book has applicability regardless of the size of your operation, and regardless of whether your operation is internal or external.

Contact or call center: What's in a name?

Traditionally, contact centers have been called call centers. The newer name — contact center — reflects the fact that more than just phone calls are being handled. Many call centers have evolved over the years to do much more than just answer phones.

Bottom line, it's up to the customer to decide how they want to communicate with your company, and it's up to your company to respond appropriately through its contact center.

Some companies choose to separate the handling of customer contacts by medium. For instance, a company may establish a department for inbound calls, one for outbound calls, and a group for e-mail. (There are as many organizational permutations as there are ways to communicate.) Some companies, especially smaller ones, opt to create "universal agents" who handle all contact types. Companies create universal contact agents for reasons of efficiency and service, and often because they find it easier to train agents in multiple communication methods than to train multiple agents in product or service information.

This book is called *Contact Centers For Dummies*. It could just as easily be called *Call Centers For Dummies*. Throughout, you'll find references to handling contacts or contact centers. Fortunately, the techniques shared and considerations discussed apply equally well to contact centers and call centers. After all, call centers can rightly be viewed as a subset of the more encompassing contact center.

The bottom line is to discover ways you can best reach out and contact your customers (or respond to them reaching out to you). Those companies that successfully communicate with customers are companies who are turned to again and again in an ever-toughening marketplace.

Figuring Out What Makes a Good Contact Center

In general, the things that make a good contact center are also the same things that make a good business. For instance, a good contact center has a strong culture where people work from a common set of values and beliefs and are bound by a common purpose and a strong focus on the business objectives. Just as in any business, effective management continually aligns everything the contact center does with its business objectives and desired culture.

Generally, as Figure 1-1 illustrates, you should look for your contact center to deliver in three areas:

- ✔ **Revenue generation:** includes everything that leads to revenue—sales, upgrades, customer retention, collections, and winning back previously lost customers.

- ✔ **Efficiency:** refers to cost-effective operations for the organization—whether this relates to the operation of the contact center or to getting work done for the organization. Generally, the contact center is a much more efficient means of contacting customers about a new promotion than John, Betty, and Fred in the marketing department.

- ✔ **Customer satisfaction:** is really long-term revenue generation—build customer loyalty and keep them doing business with you. Contact centers should make things easy for the customer. The contact center is available when the customer needs it and has access to all the information necessary to answer customer questions or solve customer problems. Try calling a checkout clerk or even the president of your favorite sporting goods store—trust me, even if you do get through, you probably won't get the answers you need.

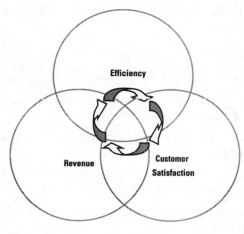

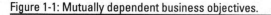

Figure 1-1: Mutually dependent business objectives.

 It's a mistake to think that revenue, efficiency, and customer satisfaction are distinct goals. In fact, they're very much mutually dependent (Figure 1-1 illustrates this). Good revenue generation cannot happen without some level of efficiency, and only satisfied customers will continue to buy a product. And, for customers to remain satisfied, they want the same thing contact centers do when they do business — an efficient transaction. For most customers, talking to your contact center is not the highlight of their day!

When a contact center fails to sell a customer on the first attempt, revenue isn't maximized because customers who really want your service/product must call back. This creates inefficiency by duplication of effort. It also represents poor service, as it makes customers do more work to get what they wanted when they initiated the first call.

The good

Not all contact centers are created equal — some are run very well with clearly defined missions, while others are a hodge-podge of people tucked away in a corner trying to poke their fingers in the dike. (Think of the brave work of Hans Brinker in saving his city in Holland.)

When everything is working as it should, a good contact center:

- ✔ Focuses on its business goals

- ✔ Answers customer contacts (phone calls, e-mails, and so on) quickly

- ✔ Has high employee morale

- ✔ Resolves a high percentage of customer inquiries on the first contact

- ✔ Measures customer satisfaction as a service indicator and has high customer satisfaction scores

- ✔ Provides a significant source of revenue for the organization

- ✔ Has a good process for collecting and presenting performance data: everyone knows where they stand monthly, daily, hourly, or in real time

- ✔ Is efficient — little rework is required: calls are consistent in length, requiring a minimum of customer time for resolution

- ✔ Has everyone engaged and busy with a purpose, but with no one overly taxed

- ✔ Improves processes continually to make constant gains in service, efficiency, and revenue generation

- ✔ Is seen corporately as a strategic advantage — an ally to the rest of the organization

Many contact centers are exemplary in their dedication to customers and clients. The real pros in the industry have transformed perceptions so that well-run contact centers are no longer viewed as "money holes" or "necessary evils," but as profit centers or a real competitive advantage.

In fact, today entire companies are built around contact center capabilities. For example, you may buy a computer from a company that doesn't have a retail store, or do your banking with a bank that doesn't have branches — they offer the telephone or Internet as your only contact options.

Legalities are important

In the United States, overly aggressive telemarketing practices have resulted in laws governing telephone sales, especially who can and cannot be contacted. These laws have affected the way that outbound contact centers can do their work.

Inbound centers are similarly touched by the law. Some industries are legislated as to how quickly they must answer incoming calls—a response to poor service and long delays that consumers have experienced in the past.

Additionally, privacy legislation has added a level of complexity to how contact centers collect and use identifying and financial information about their customers. Other legislation that restricts how and where contact centers can operate is being considered in a number of countries.

Some of the legislative challenges faced by contact centers have been brought on by poor business practices, some by the success of the industry. Explosive demand for contact center services, both from business and consumers, has taxed the discipline's ability to grow in size and capability while maintaining excellence. Still, on balance, contact centers continue to advance in number, capability, sophistication, and excellence for two reasons: They are effective and efficient business tools, and they satisfy the increasing customer demand for convenience.

If your business is running a contact center or thinking of starting a contact center, make sure you fully investigate any of the legalities involved. Legalities are important, and you don't want to land on the wrong side of a legal battle.

The bad (and the ugly)

Not all of the changes in contact centers have been viewed as positive. Contact centers and their managers have faced significant challenges. Partially because of the impact that contact centers have had on everyone's daily lives, and partially because of some bad management and bad business practices, contact centers have raised the ire of consumers and caught the attention of legislators, particularly outbound centers. (See the related sidebar.)

Not all contact centers operate in ways beneficial to either themselves or the organization as a whole. These are some things you'd expect to see in a contact center that isn't working properly:

 ✔ Long delays for customers to get through to "the next available agent"

 ✔ Frequent shuffling of customers from agent to agent

 ✔ Customers often left on hold for extended periods of time

 ✔ Customer issues that frequently require multiple contacts before they are resolved

 ✔ Low employee morale and high turnover

 ✔ No way to measure customer satisfaction — or, if there is, scores are low

 ✔ A poor understanding of metrics or performance

 ✔ Harried staff running from crisis to crisis, putting out fires but not getting ahead

 ✔ A lack of improvement in working conditions

 ✔ The wider corporation grumbles about the contact center, complains about costs, and questions the results; some talk about outsourcing

Fortunately, as ugly as the symptoms of a bad contact center are, they can be solved. It takes determination and perhaps a complete "rethinking" of your organization, but solutions do exist. This book provides a few strategies, tools, and skills to help you control what your contact center produces.

As with any business, a competent and productive contact center is the result of well-planned objectives and conscientious alignment — management needs to align practices so that they are consistent with objectives. When this is done effectively, the contact center will have many characteristics of the good, few if any of the bad, and none of the ugly.

A well-run contact center is not an accident. It's a result of good planning and good execution by good people.

What Does the Future Hold?

As technology and management practices improve, so will the sophistication, capability, and service of contact centers. If it has not happened already, your contact center will likely continue to evolve, integrating all methods of communication into one quick and seamless channel, regardless of what language or device your customers are using.

One of the fascinating things about contact centers is their never-ending pursuit of improvement. Effective managers are constantly looking for better technology, better processes, better people, and better training for those people. It's all part of the original charter for contact centers: to find more effective ways of communicating with customers so the company can serve customers better and cheaper, while generating more revenue.

Accordingly, I look for contact center services to become more customized to the needs of individual customers. There will be technological advancements, perhaps some "ohhs and ahhs" in what contact centers can do with automation. But the end result will be that more contact centers will provide better service. Great one-on-one service will become the minimum expectation for doing business, regardless of the medium.

Fortunately contact centers aren't alone in their quest to better service their customers. Leading vendors, such as Avaya, continue to provide groundbreaking technology specifically tailored to the needs of a modern contact center. Such companies stand ready to partner with organizations interested in meeting the future head-on. As you read through this book you'll get a glimpse of the future and how you can plan for it.

As contact centers improve in all aspects of their operation, they will look for ways to go beyond customer service — to make the experience of dealing with the company better. Contact centers will do all of this because customers expect — and deserve — the best.

Part II

Business Basics: Models and Drivers and Goals, Oh My!

● ●

In This Chapter

▶ Developing meaningful business objectives

▶ Supporting business objectives with powerful performance drivers

▶ Establishing balance in your drivers

▶ Creating reports that help you to measure success

● ●

*T*his part takes you on a whirlwind tour through the wonderful world of business models. In the process you can discover the ins and outs of such fundamentals as business objectives, performance drivers, and touch briefly on reporting.

A business model is a high-level description of how your business is organized and what things you're going to do to produce whatever results you deem appropriate. A business model is really no more complicated than a game plan or playbook. "Our goal is to win the game, so here's what we're going to do. . . ."

Like game plans, business models change and evolve. Over time, your model will become outdated or you'll find better ways to do things, resulting in a need to modify the plan. The important thing is to *have* a plan.

Determining Your Business Objectives

In the short term, your organization establishes goals and targets it wants the contact center to achieve. These goals, often referred to as *business objectives,* flow from the larger organization all the way to individual contact center agents, as shown in Figure 2-1.

Business objectives typically measure contact center effectiveness and the organization's progress against four broad areas: cost control, revenue generation, customer satisfaction, and employee satisfaction.

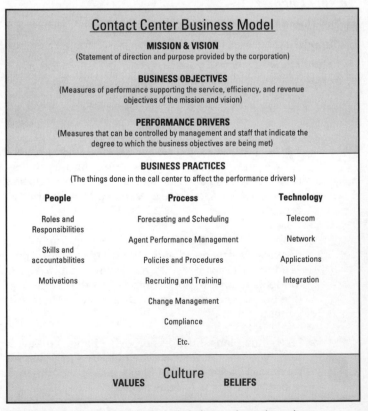

Contact Center Business Model

MISSION & VISION
(Statement of direction and purpose provided by the corporation)

BUSINESS OBJECTIVES
(Measures of performance supporting the service, efficiency, and revenue objectives of the mission and vision)

PERFORMANCE DRIVERS
(Measures that can be controlled by management and staff that indicate the degree to which the business objectives are being met)

BUSINESS PRACTICES
(The things done in the call center to affect the performance drivers)

People	**Process**	**Technology**
Roles and Responsibilities	Forecasting and Scheduling	Telecom
	Agent Performance Management	Network
Skills and accountabilities	Policies and Procedures	Applications
Motivations	Recruiting and Training	Integration
	Change Management	
	Compliance	
	Etc.	

Culture
VALUES   **BELIEFS**

Figure 2-1. Business objectives work their way down through an organization.

Remember the old phrase "Garbage in, garbage out"? Well, it rings very true with business objectives — set bad goals, and you'll get equally bad results. Business objectives need to be well thought out and justified. When well defined, these goals are the gauges that tell you about the performance of your contact center machine — like the gauges in an airplane.

Ideally you have input into specific objectives — if only to make sure that they are realistic. Specific goals and objectives vary by company, but Table 2-1 shows a few common examples.

Table 2-1 Example Contact Center Business Objectives

Goal/Objective	Measure	What It Tells Us
Customer satisfaction	Post-contact satisfaction scores Contact abandonment rate Average speed of answer	Are our agents providing good service? Are we answering contacts quickly enough? (Hanging up is one form of customer feedback!)
Cost control	Cost per contact Cost per customer Cost per case Cost per order	Are we handling contacts in an efficient manner? Do customers have to contact us too often?
Revenue generation	(Net) revenue per customer Revenue per contact	Are we making money? Are we maximizing sales and upselling opportunities? Are we growing the business?
Employee satisfaction	Employee opinion survey Retention rate Employee referrals	Do our employees feel valued and respected? Do they like working here?

Identifying a good objective

There are two important characteristics of good business objectives: They're measurable and they tell a complete story.

Ideally, a measurable objective tells you as much about an area of the business as possible. For example, using total contact center expenses to measure cost control tells you something about what the center costs to run, but it really doesn't tell you if it's profitable or not. A contact center that costs $1 million per year but has only one customer is much more expensive than a contact center that costs $50 million but has millions of customers.

The following are some good parameters for measuring objectives:

- ✓ **Revenue per customer:** the total revenue generated by the contact center divided by the number of customers

- ✓ **Cost per customer:** the total cost of running the contact center divided by total number of customers

- ✓ **Customer satisfaction:** how satisfied customers are with their contact center experience

- ✓ **Employee job satisfaction:** how satisfied contact center employees are with their jobs

Really, you can find or create all kinds of measures — as long as they tell you what you want to know about your operation.

Avoiding misleading measures

When considering business objectives, some common contact center measures should be avoided simply because they don't tell the complete story and, as such, can be misleading.

An example is the operating budget — how much your company spends to run the contact center. Most companies would like to minimize the total cost of running their center, but if the company is growing at 50 or 100 percent per year, then in all likelihood contact center costs are going to rise. So looking at the contact center budget can be misleading when considering cost control.

Another example is cost per contact — a very common measure that is simply the cost of running a contact center for a period of time divided by the contacts answered for the same period. Cost per contact can be misleading because it doesn't consider the impact of poor quality and repeat contacts. If agents don't do a good job handling customer contacts, then they are bound to call back. Although your cost per contact may appear low, a large number of repeats increases your cost per customer.

Measuring Progress with Performance Drivers

Business objectives are derived from your mission and are the goals and targets you're trying to achieve. Using them to manage your contact center requires that you understand and use performance drivers.

Performance drivers are processes and behaviors — expressed as measures — that influence achieving your business objectives. For example, average contact length is a driver of contact center costs and has a direct impact on the business objective of cost per customer. So, average contact length is a driver of cost.

Performance drivers are the building blocks of the operation, and with them you can mathematically model the business objectives, budgets, and other aspects of operations — creating the economic model of your contact center.

Drop by a contact center and you're likely to hear discussions about some of these performance drivers:

- ✔ **Service level:** refers to how fast you answer the phone, e-mail messages, and so on. It is most commonly measured by the percentage of incoming contacts answered in a specified amount of time. For example, if the contact center answers 78 percent of all contacts within 30 seconds, the service level achieved is 78/30.

- ✔ **Average contact length:** refers to how long it takes, on average, to process one customer interaction.

✔ **Agent availability:** tells you how many of your agents are actually available to take a call — that is, they're not already busy on a call.

✔ **Agent occupancy:** refers to the percentage of time that agents are busy with customers.

✔ **Conversion rates:** the percentage of contacts converted to sales (customer saves).

✔ **Retention rates:** how many potentially lost customers were saved by agents.

✔ **Customer satisfaction:** how satisfied your customers are with the level of service your contact center's providing.

✔ **First-contact resolution:** the percentage of customers who do not have to try back within a certain time frame (usually a day) to have their issue resolved.

Categorizing the drivers

Generally, performance drivers can be grouped into four areas. There are drivers that affect

✔ cost control

✔ customer satisfaction

✔ revenue generation

✔ employee satisfaction

Each category is discussed in the following sections.

Cost-control drivers

Your contact center is likely to come under the microscope for cost control often, even though contact centers are on average an efficient way to communicate with customers. Still, contact center expenditures are frequently one of the larger budgetary line items for corporations, so it's no wonder their costs are scrutinized.

Items that affect the cost control of your contact center include

✔ contact length

✔ agent occupancy

✔ average cost of putting an agent online (wages, benefits, overhead, and so on)

✔ repeat contacts from customers who don't get an accurate or complete answer on the first try

✔ nonproductive agent time (time away from the phone)

Well-run contact centers dig deep into these aspects of operations to better understand why they achieve the levels they do and how to affect them in the future. For example, contact length can be broken down into time spent communicating with the customer and post-contact work (time spent processing customer requests after the customer is gone). Both can be better understood when looking at how long different types of contacts take — an information contact versus a sales contact, for example.

Revenue drivers

It don't mean a thing if you ain't got ka-ching! Improving revenue generation can have a greater impact on margins than improvements in cost-control measures. In larger contact centers, small improvements in the customer retention rate represent hundreds of thousands or even millions of dollars in saved revenue. Similarly, small improvements in selling and upselling can have a big bottom-line impact.

In addition to your retention rate, key revenue metrics you need to consider include

✔ conversion rate (the number of sales made per contacts handled)

✔ revenue generated per sale

✔ cancellations per contact (a variation on retention rate)

✔ revenue lost per cancellation (a measure of the degree to which individual agents are mitigating revenue loss)

Customer-satisfaction drivers

Your customers want the same thing you do — an efficient and professional resolution to their problem. That's the primary reason that the metrics to measure and drive service include

✔ How fast you satisfy the customer's request— including average speed of answer, service level, and hold time.

✔ Number of times a customer needs to be transferred to another agent or representative

✔ Contact review assessments — are your agents being professional, courteous, and competent?

Employee-satisfaction drivers

Get to know your employees so you can determine what the drivers to their satisfaction are. Some things that almost certainly come up as key drivers to satisfaction include

✔ **Supervisor support:** Am I getting the help that I need?

✔ **Fairness:** Is the workload distributed equitably so that I am not too busy while other agents are idle?

✔ **Feedback:** Do I know where I stand?

✔ **Training:** Did I get the training that I need to do the job well?

The importance of balance

You'll need balance to maximize each component of performance and provide the best solution for achieving your business objectives. When you're attempting to strike this balance, keep in mind that overemphasis on one area can hurt performance in others. For example, too much emphasis on cost control can hurt service and revenue.

Don't go overboard on cost control

You've taken your quest for cost control too far if you

✔ Hire low-cost people otherwise unsuited for the job.

✔ Skimp on training and feedback.

✔ Don't spend adequately on support services.

Avoid a surplus of service

Customer service is crucial, but making the customer like you shouldn't be your only goal. Remember that customers want contact center agents to perform a service, not become their best pals.

Ensuring that ten agents are always available, waiting for the next call, to answer every customer call inside the first ring might be overly expensive. Your average customer is probably okay with waiting an average of three rings before their call is answered.

Resist revenue-generation mania

It can really turn off a long-term customer with a service concern if an agent fails to resolve the issue but makes great attempts to close in for more sales.

Although an overall focus on revenue generation is vital, overemphasizing short-term revenue gain will probably lead to long-term service pain, as your contact center loses the lifetime value of a loyal customer.

Don't focus on entertaining employees

When it comes to making employees happy, some companies live with the motto, "Try not to upset anyone." If you adopt that motto you'll probably end up hurting your contact center's performance.

People need feedback, and sometimes feedback is negative. Over time a fair, honest, and consistent approach wins as much or more in morale as does a soft hand — and it has the added benefit of keeping the organization on track.

For good contact center operation, try to strike a perfect balance between cost control, revenue generation, customer satisfaction, and employee satisfaction.

Table 2-2 provides a summary of the basic contact center business goals and the corresponding key performance drivers that affect them.

Table 2-2   Contact Center Business Objectives and the Performance Drivers That Affect Them

Objectives	Measured By	Driven By (Performance Drivers)
Cost control	Cost per contact	Contact length Cost per hour of providing the service

Table 2-2 *(continued)*

Objectives	Measured By	Driven By (Performance Drivers)
		Percentage of time agents spend with customers Percentage of contacts resolved on first attempt
Revenue generation	Revenue per customer	Percentage of contacts resulting in a sale Dollar value of sales made
Customer satisfaction	Post-contact customer satisfaction survey	Accessibility Agent professionalism, courtesy, ability Process — ability to service the customer
Employee satisfaction Employee turnover	Employee opinion score	Management behavior and support — especially direct supervisor Adequate training Consistent feedback

Reporting: Providing Feedback

Contact centers are data factories. Almost every tool that a contact center agent uses collects, stores, and reports on something. Used properly, this information provides contact center managers with tremendous intelligence to analyze performance, develop practices resulting in improvements, and discard practices that don't support objectives.

Increasingly, contact centers are hiring analysts with advanced degrees in statistics and engineering because their findings are so valuable in what they offer via improvements through the business model.

Reporting completes the contact center business model. Information reports give managers feedback they need about whether their practices and performance drivers are properly aligned with the contact center's business objectives.

Part III

The Master Plan: Finance, Analysis, and Resource Management

● ●

In This Chapter

▶ Managing business objectives

▶ Managing performance drivers

▶ Establishing targets for performance

▶ Focusing on resource management

▶ Setting staff schedules

● ●

*P*rudence dictates that contact center managers pay close attention to finance, analysis, and resource management. Contact centers can be complex beasts and they run very much by the numbers, so all three items play a significant role in operating them effectively.

Miniscule changes in procedures can make an enormous difference in results, including — and especially — performance and financial results. Increasingly, contact center managers are turning to analysts to help identify improvement opportunities.

Understanding and improving performance isn't just the concern of analysts. Ideally, everyone in the center is concerned with performance and the numbers. This part includes basic information that should be understood and practiced by as many people in the center as possible.

Business-Objective Measurements

Business objectives are the desired outputs of the contact center—what the corporation needs from the contact center by way of revenue generation, cost management, and customer satisfaction (see Part II for more about setting business objectives).

In the following sections you find some common ways to measure whether your contact center business objectives are being met.

Contact Center operating budget

The operating budget is the sum of all the costs associated with running a contact center for a given period, usually a year. The largest cost in the contact center budget is typically labor. In traditional contact centers, it is not unusual to base budgets on common assumptions, such as the number of contacts that the center will receive, how long those contacts will last, and what it takes to achieve resolution on the contacts. These assumptions are used to determine staffing needs and to anticipate other costs.

Companies need operating budgets, and managing a budget can help the company achieve its goals. Very effective contact center managers have a great deal of control over their costs and can generally tell you how much they'll spend in any month—long before the finance department produces an expense report.

By understanding the factors that go into your budget, you can play "what if" with those factors to see the bottom-line effect. Being able to do a quick calculation on the impact of changing the drivers goes a long way to motivating management to find ways to make improvements.

Cost center versus profit center

Many times management views a contact center as a burdensome expense for the corporation. This may not be a fair assessment, however, because many contact centers turn out to be profit centers — they help create customer loyalty and generate sales that may otherwise have been lost.

You can pay attention to a number of measurements on the cost side of any equation, including the following:

- ✔ **Cost per contact.** Calculated by dividing the total costs to run the contact center for a period of time by the total contacts responded to in the same period.

- ✔ **Cost per customer.** Calculated by dividing the total cost of running the contact center for a period of time by the average number of customers for the same time frame.

- ✔ **Cost per resolution.** Divide total costs for the period by the cases resolved, looking for improvement over time.

These are obviously very simplistic measurements, and will suffice for some contact centers. Others use more complex measurements that either build on or entirely replace these simplistic ones. Many of the measurements you should pay attention to are provided by the management applications used at your site; make sure you review what is available and determine which measurements fit best with your needs.

On the profit center side of the coin you can utilize entirely different measurements, such as:

- ✔ **Total revenue generation.** Your finance or marketing department will calculate total revenue generated.

- ✔ **Revenue per contact.** Divide total revenue generated during a period of time by the number of contacts for the same period.

- ✔ **Revenue per customer.** Divide the total revenue generated for a period of time by the average number of customers over the same time frame.

If you can constantly reduce cost per customer and increase revenue per customer, then you're looking the good life right in the eye — corner office, parking space, key to the executive lunchroom — it's all yours!

One way that you can help decrease costs — while still handling more volume — is through the implementation of self-service technologies. Part IV introduces some of these technologies, such as IVR and speech-enabled systems, which enable customers to help themselves rather than tying up valuable (and costly) agent time.

Paying for it all

Those charged with overseeing the finances of an operation must always be concerned with one overriding question: How does the company pay for it all? In other words, how do you generate the revenue necessary to cover the expenses inherent in any contact center?

This is a fundamental question, and one that you need to ask often. You can go far toward answering the question by transforming, if at all possible, your contact center into a revenue source. Look for ways that you can upsell, cross-sell, and just plain sell. Chances are good that your contacts have a problem (why else would they be contacting you?) and any salesperson knows that problems are synonymous with opportunities.

Just because you see a customer problem as an opportunity doesn't mean that the customer has the same vision. Make sure you are sensitive to resolving the customer's needs, and don't be overbearing in trying to sell.

Performance Drivers: Managing the Results

Performance drivers are variables that have an impact on your contact center's business objectives (see Part II for more detail). They're called performance drivers because, like a person who manages the controls of a car, or like the programs that make computer equipment work, drivers are things that make other things go. In this case, performance drivers make business objectives go.

Performance drivers are often different based on the method in which contacts are realized. For instance, performance drivers are different for phone contacts when compared to e-mail contacts, and completely different from contacts handled through self-service methods or IVR. (See Part IV for information on contact center technologies.) As you consider adjusting drivers to change your results, make sure you take into account the contact methods. This may mean examining different reports and establishing different tracking methods, but your results will be better when you take all information into account.

Examining performance drivers

A key component to controlling and manipulating outcomes is to designate responsibility throughout the organization — most importantly to the contact center agents, because each agent is a microcosm of the operation.

Table 3-1 shows how to track and improve results on the agent level. Individual agent improvement pulls up improvement in overall average agent performance, which in turn drives overall improvement in the contact center.

Table 3-1	Measures at the Agent Level
Contact Center Drivers	*Agent-Level Drivers*
Cost per hour of agent time	Wage rate
Agent utilization	Schedule adherence
Call length	Call length
Contacts per customer	
First-Call Resolution	First-Call Resolution
Occupancy	N/A
Conversion per contact	Conversion per contact
Dollar value per conversion	Dollar value per conversion
Accessibility	N/A

One of the first things you notice in Table 3-1 is that some contact center measures do not correlate with agent-level measures, since agents cannot directly influence those measures. For example, occupancy and service level are group measures that individual agents cannot control, although individual agents' ability and professionalism contribute to the group measures. However, if you implement some segmentation method, such as Direct Agent Calls, that enables customers to always get their favorite agent, you may be able to improve overall measures for the contact center.

You may also notice that cost per hour becomes wage rate at the agent level, because only the wage rate directly correlates to the individual agent; all other costs are for the entire contact center.

 Probably hundreds of performance drivers can impact a contact center's results. A big part of an analyst's job is to identify these relationships and gain a better understanding of how the relationships between business objectives and performance drivers work.

Call-oriented metrics

Any number of performance drivers may be related to calls or other contacts. You can get a better handle on them by examining the measurements related to calls and contacts. The following sections detail some of the more common call-oriented metrics.

Call length

Call length is one of the most powerful measures in the contact center. It's a little controversial in that some believe too much focus is put on call length without appropriate attention to other measures. However, customers want the same thing that contact centers do — a quick, accurate, and complete resolution to their problem or inquiry. In general, shorter call times mean everyone is happier.

 A longer call can be a wonderful thing if it brings more revenue per minute. For example, if a customer gets a question resolved quickly and is so pleased with the service that he orders more product, the extra minute of tender loving care the agent provides may well result in one-call resolution and repeat business.

Contacts per customer

Contacts per customer is another useful measure for forecasting and tracking contact center cost control over time. Tracking the number of contacts per customer on a monthly or daily basis and then multiplying that by the current number of customers gives a very useful forecast of call volume.

Don't rely solely on an average contacts per customer statistic to do your forecasting. You need to factor in other data points as well, such as historical "busy periods," such as holidays, along with any campaign and market changes.

Conversion per contact

Let me make sure I'm clear here. A *contact* is any time you say hello (via the phone, self-service, e-mail, chat, whatever). A *conversion* is any time you generate or save revenue on a contact. Conversion per contact affects total revenue generated and other revenue objectives.

Accessibility

Accessibility means how easy it is for a person to make contact — it's how fast you're answering the phone, e-mail, or letter. It's important because it has an impact on customer satisfaction and cost control. Here are three common measures of the many used to calculate accessibility:

- ✔ **Service level:** Refers to the percentage of callers whose calls are answered within a defined time.

- ✔ **Average speed of answer:** Also known as ASA, this refers to the average amount of time your customers waited in queue before an agent greeted them.

- ✔ **Abandonment rate:** The percentage of callers that hang up before an agent responds to their contact attempt.

Agent professionalism and ability

Agent ability is probably the most important requirement in achieving customer nirvana. Whether calling a contact center or shopping for new shoes, most customers expect the same thing of the customer-service people they deal with: know what you're talking about, and be nice!

Customer satisfaction surveys can help in this regard. Through the surveys, customers can tell you about the agents who aren't nice or who can't do their job. When you ask the right questions, customers will also tell you specifically what your company needs to improve at.

 Many contact centers have people listen to agent calls to determine if they are professional and capable; this is frequently referred to as "call assessment" or "call monitoring." The evaluator scores the agent calls against a template of key call behaviors.

First-Call Resolution

First-Call Resolution (FCR) refers to the percentage of customer inquiries completed on the first attempt. If customers have to call back once or many times because the contact center did not resolve their inquiry or concern the first time, then FCR will decline — and so will customer satisfaction.

The benefits of tracking First-Call Resolution are large. Improving this measure has an impact on customer satisfaction. It also improves cost control — improving First-Call Resolution reduces the load on a contact center as the number of repeat calls decreases.

Policies and procedures

The drivers listed so far in this part aren't the only ones that influence your operation. A large part of your analyst's job is learning how to identify and manipulate these and other drivers of contact center performance. After she has identified the variables that contribute to performance, she'll look to your company and contact center policies and procedures to understand the process behind each driver.

Setting Performance Targets

Setting performance targets is extremely important. People work better with very specific targets, whereas vague targets create vague results. When setting performance targets, you first have to figure out what's the right thing to target. You then have to determine what level of performance to expect for that target. This section provides some ideas that can help you set appropriate targets for some of the most important contact center drivers.

Accessibility/service level

Here are some examples of methods you can use to set performance targets for service level:

- ✔ **Do what everyone else does.** The default level of service for answering phone calls tends to be 80/20 (80 percent of calls are answered in 20 seconds or less). E-mail and chat don't seem to have generally accepted standards, perhaps because of their relative infancy.

- ✔ **Go with the industry direction.** A number of industries are self-regulated or even government-regulated in terms of how fast contact centers must answer the phone.

- ✔ **Develop a business case.** Do a cost-benefit analysis to determine your service-level objective. Evaluate each of your customer segments for tolerance levels for waiting in queue. For example, you may notice that for your premier customer group, the number of abandons spikes sharply after 15 seconds, whereas the tolerance level for a general help line is much higher. If you do this analysis well, you can find the break-even point between the cost of providing faster service and the benefit of providing that service.

Abandons

Abandons are defined as customers who try to contact your business, but fail to reach an agent for one reason or another. The most common type of abandon is a customer who hangs up before an agent is available to answer the call. Abandons also occur in other contact methods (e-mail, chat, and so on), but are easiest to track on phone contacts.

You want to reduce abandons as much as possible. You won't get rid of them all, since some are completely out of your control, such as someone who has dialed a wrong number. You do, however, want to minimize those you can. It is best to view abandons as a measure of customer satisfaction. If your customers are abandoning a lot, they don't like the speed of your service. Speed up your service, and your abandons should drop.

One way that some companies have helped decrease abandons is to implement a self-service system that answers the most common customer queries, without the need to involve an agent. Self-service does away with the necessity of placing a customer on hold, so customer satisfaction can be improved even while abandon rates are dropping.

Call length

It's difficult to come up with the proper benchmark for call length because there are too many variables that go into the mix. Product complexity, system capabilities, responsiveness, working environment, information collected via self-service, training, and a host of other variables can affect call length. Identifying the one *right* call length is nearly impossible.

What you can — and should — do is try to understand as much about your own center's (or, more accurately, each of its own individual campaigns') call length as possible. Of course, you can also attempt to make call length as consistent as possible. Ideally you should also measure the impact of a call. For instance, does a longer call result in more revenue for the company? If so, then the agent should not be penalized for longer call lengths.

Occupancy

Occupancy — how busy your agents are with current contacts — is an important measure of whether you are efficiently using agents. If your agent occupancy is consistently very high, you could be causing agent burn-out. On the other hand, if occupancy is too low, this unused agent time is adding significantly to your costs.

CASE STUDY

Calling all cost-effective contact center solutions

Here's a modern dilemma: Who do you call when your cell phone doesn't work? A cellular service provider needs superior contact center response time and efficiency to keep customers from hanging up — permanently. When one company needed to improve contact center efficiency, it called Avaya.

Operating under the well-known BeeLine brand, VimpelCom is one of Russia's three leading cellular service companies and the first Russian company listed on the New York Stock Exchange. The company was formed in 1992; today VimpelCom's GSM network serves more than 10 million customers, including more than 5 million in the Moscow area. Its licenses cover some 92 percent of the Russian population.

A clear call to improve customer service

Like customers everywhere, cellular subscribers in Russia demand advanced products, competitive pricing and, most of all, great customer service. VimpelCom's subscribers value the company's innovative marketing and high quality service and customer care.

It hasn't always been that way, however. When the company established its first contact center in 1995, responsiveness to callers did not meet VimpelCom's goal to provide stellar customer service. Within five years, some customers were facing lengthy wait times — as long as 15 to 20 minutes. Finding a solution to improve its responsiveness to customers quickly became a top priority for VimpelCom.

VimpelCom's commitment to customer care led the company to build its network of seven contact centers. They decided to implement Avaya DEFINITY Servers in each contact center, expanding quickly from 200 operators in 2000 to more than 900 operators today.

VimpelCom's Avaya-powered contact centers now handle more than 45 million calls each month — nine times the volume of five years ago. Average customer wait times have been dramatically reduced, with more than half of customer calls answered in 30 seconds or less, and average call handling time down by 75 percent. Three out of four customers now express satisfaction with the service they receive.

Following a clear improvement path

In 2001 VimpelCom added more support for its operators by implementing Avaya Interactive Voice Response (IVR) at the major Moscow contact center. By enabling callers to route their own calls and access recorded

(continued)

(continued)

information, Avaya IVR continues to help VimpelCom operators focus on the most significant customer issues and boost productivity.

VimpelCom also realized that the quality contact center solution it sought would require the best support as well as the best products. The company engaged Avaya Global Services to implement the transition to the new Avaya solution. VimpelCom also used Avaya Global Services to provide contact center consultants who developed the needed scripting for the IVR application.

Other enhancements have followed. The Avaya Call Management System provides up-to-date status on contact center operations and helps managers react and plan for high customer service. Operator productivity and attrition rates have improved with NICE Systems call recording for training and development of operators.

Today, VimpelCom relies on Avaya contact center solutions across all seven of its regional contact centers. Callers wait just seconds for service, and contact center managers rely on a rich flow of information and reports to keep operators and workloads in balance.

When your actual service level is too high above the target, it's costing you too much in labor. If it's too far below the target it's costing you customer satisfaction, revenue, and other expenses. Cost control is balanced when service level is right on the target.

Understanding Resource Management Tasks and Concepts

Okay, relax — this won't hurt a bit. You need this stuff and it's easy. This is an overview of the key concepts and tools used in contact center resource management — important for scheduling.

Forecasting

Forecasting refers to predicting the future — specifically, how much work your center is going to have. The key is to accurately determine your workload and when you'll have it, so you can match resources to demand.

Don't assume that the time it takes to process calls, e-mails, or Web chats is always the same. It makes sense that a very simple customer inquiry is likely to take much less time to process on average than a complicated, high-level technical support call. Contact length will fluctuate over time, as will call volume.

Scheduling

Scheduling is the process of assigning resources to meet your demand. Where forecasting provides the "how much" part of resource management, scheduling answers the "who, what, where, and when" parts. An important part of managing the contact center is providing schedules that are workable and help achieve business objectives. Some centers go so far as to measure *schedule adherence,* which reflects whether agents adhered to the schedule that was implemented.

Full-time equivalent

Usually referred to by the short form FTE, *full-time equivalent* is a way to express how many people you need to schedule. Staffing requirements are expressed in terms of the number of people working full-time hours. For instance, one FTE may equal 7.5 paid hours. So, if call demand required 750 total paid hours to get the work done for a day, this would equate to 100 FTEs.

Real-time management of resources

As the name suggests, real-time resource management refers to making the necessary ongoing changes from your original schedule based on real-life, up-to-the-minute changes in call volume and staff availability so that your contact center achieves the best possible results each day.

Assigning Staff and Creating Schedules That Work

Sooner or later you get to the point where you need to attach the names of the agents who will work the shifts. The easiest way is for you to simply pick names and assign them to a schedule — if, that is, you really don't want people to like you.

Probably the safest (and fairest) way, especially in larger contact centers, is to post the schedules and allow staff to bid on the available shifts, giving bidding priority to senior staff members.

Some contact centers use alternatives to shift bids. These might include rotating staff through all shifts (essentially, sharing the pain), working around employees' personal preferences, assignment by employee performance, or fixed permanent shifts.

Regardless of the approach, you're bound to have less than desirable shifts. This can be somewhat demoralizing for staff, considering that the majority of folks would rather be working 9 to 5, Monday to Friday. Some things you can do to ease their angst include:

- ✔ **Re-bidding:** Redoing the schedule from time to time is a good idea. It allows your staff to move up the chain and get more-desirable shifts, and can really improve team motivation.

- ✔ **Shift-trading:** Give your employees a mechanism for trading their shifts — "You work my 9 to 5 and I'll work your 1 to 9." It's usually done on a one-day-at-a-time basis.

- ✔ **Time bank/flex time:** Allow employees the option to *bank* extra hours they work and take them as time off at a future date. This approach works well if it's administered and tracked carefully.

Part IV

Making It Go: An Introduction to Contact Center Technology

*B*roadly speaking, technology does three things for your contact center:

✔ It gives your customers a way to communicate with your company.

✔ It enables the contact center to more readily collect, access, and edit information about your customers.

✔ It provides a means for reporting on activity within your contact center.

Contact center technology is becoming increasingly integrated — making for improved processes and resulting in increases in customer satisfaction, efficiency, and revenue generation.

The Need for Appropriate Technology

Contact centers are a response to the demand for convenience in a world that continues to move faster. Consumers don't have the time or desire to go to the market square for every purchase or to receive services. Technology helps customers process transactions and obtain information more quickly and accurately, and is the foundation upon which contact centers are built.

Running your contact center, however, is still about people and processes. Good operations blend people, processes, and technology into effective solutions that maximize customer satisfaction, cost control, and revenue generation. They maximize the lifetime value of the relationship. When you apply proper technology to a well-thought-out contact center plan, you can build an effective business solution.

Figure 4-1 shows the basic layout of a typical contact center network, illustrating many of the pieces of technology discussed in this part.

Getting the Customer to the Contact Center

Most customer contact is handled through the phone. Agents spend a huge portion of their day fielding calls from customers and providing resolution to problems or issues. Today's telephone networks provide your contact center with a number of valuable services described in the following sections.

Automatic Number Identification

Automatic Number Identification (ANI) transmits the customer's telephone number and delivers it to your contact center's telephone system. In residential service, ANI is often referred to as *caller ID*.

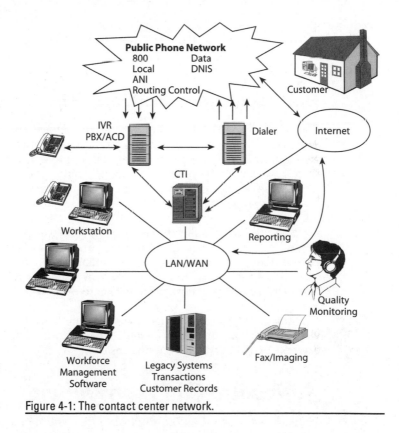

Figure 4-1: The contact center network.

ANI can be very valuable because the calling number information can be used to identify customers and look up account
information before an agent even says hello. You can use this
information to give the caller special treatment — your very
best customers might be routed to an elite group of agents,
for example. Special routing is a great way to boost customer
satisfaction and revenue per customer.

Dialed Number Identification Service (DNIS)

Because your contact center probably has several different
incoming numbers — depending on the various services or
products you offer — it's important for you to know which of
those numbers the customer called. Through Dialed Number

Identification Service (DNIS) the telephone network provides you with the number that the customer dialed. This information tells the telephone system how to route the caller.

Dynamic network routing

This service goes by a number of different names, but the basic concept remains the same. Some contact centers have a computer that is directly connected to the telephone company's switching office. This computer enables you to control the routing of your customer's calls at the network level — before they hit your telephone system.

For example, when call volumes peak beyond a level that can be serviced in your center, you can redirect calls to other centers that you have overflow agreements with. Calls can be routed based on a number of different criteria, such as a predetermined percentage allocation to each office.

 Dynamic network routing also gives you one method of providing call-prompting (press 1 for English, 2 for Spanish, for example) right in the telephone network.

Automatic Call Distribution

Think of Automatic Call Distribution (ACD) as the heart of the contact center. When customer calls arrive, they are delivered to the ACD — a phone system that routes a large volume of incoming calls to a pool of waiting agents. It's different from other phone systems in that it makes use of telephone queues instead of extensions. (A queue acts as sort of a waiting room for callers.) ACD has a number of important capabilities:

- ✔ **Announcements (delay messaging):** This is the recording that says, "Thank you for calling; all of our operators are currently busy . . ." or whatever polite message you want to convey.

- ✔ **Music on hold:** Music on hold plays between delay messages. Again, the main objective of music is to encourage customers to wait for the next agent.

- ✔ **Skills-based routing:** As a variation on routing to queues, most ACDs have the ability to route to skills instead. As the name suggests, skills-based routing is used to match each caller's needs with the agent who has the best skill set (of those available at the moment) to service those needs.

Predictive dialing

A predictive dialer is a device used to manage and launch large volumes of *outbound* calls. The dialer increases agent productivity by placing more outbound calls than the available number of agents. The dialer then sorts out answering machines, busy signals, and other non-human interactions before delivering live calls to the agents.

Predictive dialers can also be a great boon for contacting a customer base with information about new products or services, or to provide reminders about appointments.

Predictive dialing can increase agent productivity by 300 percent or more over manual dialing by removing list administration from the agent and reducing agent wait time between live calls. If implemented properly, customers won't even know that they are being contacted through a predictive dialing system. The best systems deliver outbound calls to agents immediately when a customer answers, without a bothersome delay that can cause a customer to hang up.

It's best to also scrub lists based on other information you may have about a customer's interest in the product or service being offered. By scrubbing out customers who are less likely to want a product that you are promoting, you increase the quality or effectiveness of your list and make more sales over the life of the list. As a result, dialing becomes more effective.

Most countries have tabled or enacted legislation targeted at contact center practices. These laws are generally directed toward telephone sales, the use of predictive dialers, and privacy. For example, the United States has implemented legislation that requires contact centers to scrub their telemarketing lists against government-provided "do not call" lists. By checking every list against both government lists and your own internal do not call list, you can be sure that you aren't calling customers who prefer not to be called.

Getting Information to the Agent

The two most important devices for your contact center agents (or managers) are the phone and the computer. The phone routes a call from the customer's house, cell phone, or office to one of your skilled agents.

After the call is routed to an agent, that agent needs the best possible tools and resources to provide the customer with quick and accurate service. Today's networked computer systems are the means by which your agents access these capabilities, which include customer accounts and product or service information and pricing.

More sophisticated environments also include access to a wide range of information:

- Company knowledge bases including problem-solving guidelines, policies, and procedures
- Call guides and scripts, sometimes including dynamic scripts that customize call-handling recommendations based on individual customer characteristics and preferences
- A personal performance "dashboard," which provides agents with critical information pertaining to their job performance
- Communication tools for communicating with other departments, peers, and management
- Screen pop-ups of relevant customer information
- The Internet
- Other tools such as software for e-mail, chat, collaboration, faxes, and letters

The key is to provide at the agent's fingertips everything they'll need to perform their job. If this can be done with as few applications as possible, all the better.

Computer/Telephone Integration

Computer/Telephone Integration (CTI) refers to a system of hardware and software that allows for communication between the telephone system and the computer system. With this communication, you're able to instruct both systems to work together to produce some interesting and powerful applications. CTI is like contact center superglue, only better.

A common and popular CTI application is the "screen pop," in which the system collects the caller's telephone number and passes this information to the computer/telephone integration system. The CTI system then looks up the customer's information in the database. When a customer account is found, the CTI system sends the call and the customer information simultaneously to an agent's telephone and workstation. Estimates suggest that the screen pop saves 10 to 15 seconds in average call length.

Easy access to customer info by phone number is just one example of a computer/telephone integration application. Some other neat examples made possible by this technology include

- **Mandatory data entry:** CTI can be used to make the entry of critical data mandatory before agents can take the next call.

- **Coordinated screen transfer:** This function enables agents to transfer what's on the customer screen as they transfer calls to another agent or supervisor.

- **Dynamic scripting:** After the caller has been routed to an agent, CTI may prompt the agent with a customized script or call-handling approach to serve the specific customer.

- **Call blending:** Call blending occurs when agents can be switched among different types of work at any time. For example, an agent might be blended between inbound customer service calls and outbound collections.

Getting Information to the Customer

Technology is not only useful for getting information to your agents, but it can also be invaluable in getting information directly to your customer. Two main types of systems exist: automated response systems and speech-enabled systems.

Interactive Voice Response systems

Interactive Voice Response (IVR) systems are known by several names, such as Automated Response Systems (ARS) or automated attendant. The concept behind such systems is that the customer is presented with a series of choices from which he or she can choose. The choices made at any point in the call dictates the choices next presented.

The idea behind automated response is to provide a quick, efficient way for the customer to get the information needed. For instance, whenever you've called your bank to determine your credit balance and used the automated account lookup, which reads your account balance in an automated voice, you've used an IVR system.

 Automated Response Systems are very cost-effective. The cost of a service provided by IVR can be less than 20 percent the cost of providing the same service using a live agent. The payback on investing in an IVR can be very fast—well under a year.

Speech-enabled systems

Speech-enabled systems go one better than traditional automated response systems—they allow your system to recognize verbal customer commands. Traditional automated response systems accept input through touch-tones. Speech-enabled systems, however, can accept human language commands.

The immediate benefit of speech-enabled systems is that they are easier and faster for customers to use. With a larger percentage of the calling public using cell phones, it becomes cumbersome to continually look at the keypad and press a number. Speech-enabled systems allow customers to speak naturally and access the information they want.

AAA drives down costs and delivers on better service

More than 700,000 members of the American Automobile Association (AAA) of Minnesota/Iowa rely on the club for everything from emergency roadside service to affordable auto insurance to quality itinerary recommendations and discounted rates while traveling the globe. So when the club sought to centralize customer service operations, it required a self-service solution to uphold its reputation for reliability.

AAA Minnesota/Iowa has three contact centers consisting of 61 agents. The centers support membership and travel services, but automation was almost nonexistent. In fact, 99 percent of callers were being helped by live agents who manually processed all of their requests. The club wanted to offer customers more efficient service, while reducing contact center costs and ensuring that specially trained agents were more available to assist members with emergencies and travel planning.

The club faced several challenges, including how to better centralize operations, expand products and services, and train agents who could specialize in new services, all while maintaining their award-winning customer-care reputation and improving agents' job satisfaction. "Strategically we wanted to provide better customer service. We needed the ability to handle spikes in the call traffic, ensure that we had high-quality personnel, and also reduce our costs of transaction," says Joe Alessi, vice president of marketing and information technology for AAA of Minnesota/Iowa.

To reduce costs and improve customer service, the club determined that it needed to automate key functions and reduce call durations. The club now offers a state-of-the-art speech-enabled system. With a natural speech solution, club members gain 24-hour access to AAA's popular TripTik materials, ordering maps and travel guides for a cross-country drive by speaking a beginning and ending address, as well as the dates they plan to travel.

AAA of Minnesota/Iowa selected Avaya as their solutions provider; upgrading to the new S8700 platform, the IP telephony groundwork was laid for the auto club. Avaya enabled the auto club to create a single virtual contact center operation.

The speech-enabled solution that Avaya delivered is powered by the Avaya Interactive Response software platform for voice and speech applications. This implementation also features voice recognition applications custom-designed for the auto club by Nuance and Gold Systems, both members of the Avaya DevConnect program.

(continued)

(continued)

With Avaya speech self-service applications in place, club members can use natural voice commands to renew and upgrade memberships, request travel materials, get account balances, or reach specific departments. With a current volume of 650,000 calls per year, call completion times are shorter: Speech automated self-service calls take less than half the time required when speaking with a live agent.

Now that more of the club's routine member services and transactions are automated using speech, AAA's top-tier agents are free to handle more complex requests and time sensitive, critical calls. In addition, the Avaya partner Gold Systems agents' desktop application includes a "screen pop-up" with valuable customer information that helps agents provide faster service, improving both job satisfaction and the ability to increase cross-sell opportunities.

Reporting and Data: Using Various Technology Sources to Keep Score

Without reporting you have no way of knowing how good you are, if you're improving, or if you're actually getting worse. To be effective, reporting must be timely, complete, and accurate — all a lot easier said than done.

The reports you use to manage your contact center come from a variety of sources. The following are a few examples of the reports available from various systems:

- **Agent performance reports.** Typically available from your ACD system, agent performance reports, like the example shown in Figure 4-2, provide statistics on each individual agent: how long the agent took to service calls, how many calls were answered, the amount of time that the agent was logged in, and when they logged in.

- **Queue performance report.** A queue is an answering group — it represents service provided and received by a universe of callers with similar needs. Separate queues are usually set up in an ACD system for callers with different needs, such as different languages. Queue reports tell you how many people called, how fast you answered the phone, how many customers hung up, how long it took to service the average call, how many agents were logged in to the system, and so on.

✔ **Trunk performance report.** Reports about incoming telephone lines, or trunks, are helpful to ensure appropriate facility sizing and line utilization. This report, available through an ACD or predictive dialer, is great for determining how many lines you need to lease from your phone company.

✔ **IVR reports.** Automated response system reports. An IVR unit provides reports on calls received, options customers selected, the length of time customers spent using IVR services, and when they used voice response services. (Figure 4-3 shows an example report for a customer opinion survey application.)

Agent Report

QTD	(All)									
Month	(All)									
WeekEnding	(All)									
Date	(All)									
Supervisor	(All)									

TARGET					660					
AGENT	LOGGED HOURS	OCCUPANCY	CALLS ANSWERED	AVG HANDLE TIME	AVG TALK TIME	AVG WORK TIME	AVG HOLD TIME	OUTBOUND CALLS MADE	AVG OUTBOUND TIME	AVG AUX TIME
Agent 1	285.59	59.44%	1304	186	186	0.10	8.16	32	64.66	1.76
Agent 2	149.93	65.33%	684	179	171	1.99	18.21	57	77.23	7.76
Agent 3	432.24	60.08%	1652	212	202	33.18	50.65	89	59.57	5.17
Agent 4	263.42	66.52%	1099	166	166	48.38	37.26	42	15.38	1.81
Agent 5	407.09	56.96%	1454	143	143	21.71	78.22	21	127.76	274
Agent 6	355.24	60.28%	1322	193	183	4.68	36.70	85	97.68	8.34

Figure 4-2: An agent performance report.

Avoid getting caught up in the maze of contact center reports and reporting. The best solution is to combine data from the various systems to create meaningful information about your customer's experience, your drivers, and your business performance.

With all the data available to you and an automated method of pulling these data into meaningful information, you can understand how you're performing, why you're getting your results, and how you might improve performance, all giving you very strong control. The payback of being able to read performance data and to rectify issues is practically immediate.

		Avg C.S.T. (Customer						
Interval	Calls Recieved	Service Time)	1 — Very Dissatisfied	2 — Dissatisfied	3 — Neutral	4 — Satisfied	5 — Very Satisfied	Grand Total
10:00	11	153.14				1	10	11
10:30	14	142.01					14	14
11:00	10	100.90			1		5	6
11:30	17	105.79	3			2	12	17
12:00	11	142.53			1		17	18
12:30	15	162.77		1	1	3	13	18
13:00	14	124.01	2			1	23	26
13:30	15	151.68	1				17	18
14:00	11	147.48					7	7

IVR Report
Responses Results
How satisfied were you with the amount of time our representative took to process your request?

Figure 4-3: An IVR report.

Make sure your reports differentiate between self-service contacts and "live" contacts such as phone, e-mail, chat, and so on. Having the comparative data side-by-side enables you to make determinations about which contact methods are most cost-effective and how you can better adjust those methods to meet customer needs and the contact center's business objectives.

Part V

Technological Enhancements: Getting the Newest and Coolest Stuff

● ●

In This Chapter

▶ Using enhancements in technology to ensure continuous improvement

▶ Knowing how to recommend appropriate technology

● ●

As part of a strategy of continuous improvement, contact centers are always looking at cool new technologies that may provide improvements in their business practices. Okay — maybe they're not all that "cool," but they definitely make things work better!

Driving Improvement with Technology

Your contact center's analyst is primarily responsible for identifying opportunities for improvement, but everyone contributes ideas and recommendations. The manager of technology, for example, is likely to read trade journals and visit with vendors to keep abreast of new developments. He or she may come across something that may have a net improvement, and so should generally have an answer when someone asks if there's a technological solution to affect a driver in a particular way.

In this part you find some examples of technological enhancements.

IP contact centers

VoIP is the transmission of voice conversations over an IP-based data network. It represents a fundamental shift in the way that voice messages are handled when compared to traditional circuit-switched phone systems. IP Telephony is the collective set of software-based voice applications that transport voice via VoIP.

For several years, businesses large and small have been saving significant amounts of money by converting traditional voice systems to VoIP solutions. The majority of savings is realized through a simpler network infrastructure (a converged voice and data network) and avoiding costly toll calls by carrying the majority of traffic on that network. Savings are also realized through significantly simpler maintenance — moves, adds, and changes are done in minutes instead of hours or days.

Some contact centers — perhaps yours — have already made the switch to VoIP and are just beginning to realize the benefits available through such a conversion. An IP contact center leverages IP technologies to flatten and consolidate contact center infrastructure, removing expensive network charges and running many locations from one centralized set of applications (or maybe two for redundancy).

It is this "many locations" benefit that can give contact centers a competitive advantage that was never before possible. Home agents, satellite locations, outsourced resources, and resident experts are easily added as extensions to the same contact center, all while maintaining centralized management and reporting. Contact center agents at branch offices can now have affordable access to the rich suite of contact center applications because these applications no longer have to reside on site.

SIP, or *Session Initiated Protocol,* is making its way into the contact center. Using the concept of *presence,* agents can instantly see who is logged on and what work state each expert is currently in. This facilitates an agent being able to quickly invoke the help of another agent, a supervisor, or other expert to help with an answer for the tough questions — leading to fewer transfers and faster call resolution.

For contact centers, the real value of IP is realized by implementing a number of solutions made possible by the IP infrastructure. These solutions include:

✔ **Server and application consolidation.** Contact centers can radically reduce application and infrastructure complexity. The consolidation means it is not uncommon to reduce capital expenditures by 30 percent or more and ongoing maintenance and support by 15 percent. The reduction in complexity makes your center more flexible when responding to market changes.

✔ **Virtual site consolidation.** Assuming your company has contact center resources in differing locations, an IP infrastructure increases staffing efficiencies in the range of 3 percent to 8 percent by pooling agent resources across the locations.

✔ **Resource optimization.** Because you can utilize staffing wherever it is located (on site or off), IP contact centers typically reduce staffing costs by 3 percent to 9 percent and help grow revenue. It is not uncommon to also increase customer loyalty by more easily connecting the right agent to the right caller at the right time.

✔ **Globalization.** If you've thought of expanding your contact center to include off-shore resources to provide a 24-hour follow-the-sun contact center, an IP infrastructure makes such expansion possible. Contact centers can reduce operating costs by approximately 30 percent by staffing the center with high quality, low turnover, college-educated agents from developing economies.

All of these solutions can easily cost justify themselves in standalone implementations, but they become most attractive when you understand that such solutions are much easier to implement in an IP contact center than in a traditional contact center.

 Since IP technology represents a fundamental change in a contact center's technological infrastructure, a conversion is not something to be done lightly. Fortunately, leading IP partners, such as Avaya, know that you don't need to change everything at once. You can plan for an evolutionary change, over time, that enables you to realize immediate benefits without scrapping your current systems and grow into longer-term changes that poise your company for continued growth.

Agent performance monitoring

Most contact centers do a great deal of quality monitoring. In many cases, they do this by randomly listening to and grading agent contacts, often recording them using a cassette recorder. Occasionally, the supervisor (or a member of a quality team) sits beside the agent and reviews the call immediately upon its conclusion.

Other times, the supervisor may record the call remotely and review it with the agent at a later date. This method can be effective, but it has its drawbacks. Most significant is that it is very time consuming for the supervisor. Idle time between calls and the administration of storing, recording, and grading calls makes the process very inefficient. Some supervisors have claimed that they can do about one call per hour when they included feedback.

Because the process is so labor intensive, it's difficult and impractical to target specific agent needs — such as high call length, low customer opinion, poor sales, or high returns.

 For most contact centers it's beneficial to purchase an automated quality monitoring system and integrate it into your infrastructure. Doing this can dramatically increase your supervisors' productivity and enable them to provide to the agents a greater volume of feedback with more specific detail.

The system automatically captures complete agent phone calls — recording both the voice conversation and a video picture of the agents' navigation of the systems. When supervisors are ready to review agent calls, they simply log in to the system from their workstation, retrieve sample calls from the agent or service they wish to review, and begin scoring.

Scoring is also done through the system. After they're done scoring, the supervisor can e-mail the results to the agent, with comments. The agent can also retrieve and review the call. The supervisor is relieved of the administration and wait time associated with manual quality monitoring. As a result, in some contact centers using this technology, supervisor productivity has more than tripled. Because they can retrieve calls from any agent without waiting, supervisors can target individual agents and try to understand performance deficiencies that are evident from the statistical analysis.

CRM technology

Customer Relationship Management (CRM) is a business term that refers to the process of relating to your customers to maximize the length and value of that customer relationship. It involves data collection and analysis to better understand your customers' needs and wants. It also includes customized strategies for addressing unique customer needs. The whole point of CRM is to get new customers, to keep the customers you've got, and to maximize the value of the relationships you have with those customers.

The technology of CRM is diverse. However, it doesn't have to be overly complex or uncommon — especially in the beginning. Think of CRM technology in terms of four components: data collection, data management and analysis, the creation of business rules, and customer contact applications.

Companies collect data on their customers from a variety of sources, including billing systems, contact center customer contact systems, Web-based contact information, or any other point of contact. This information is used in building the CRM database.

Managing data is an important part of any CRM system. As the system collects information about individual callers, the data are stored in a large data warehouse. This information can be analyzed and inferences made about your customers' needs and intentions. You can make these inferences at the individual customer level, creating a service plan for each one.

Developing a CRM strategy

The core of any CRM strategy is to create a philosophy and plan on how you want to treat your customers, what you want to get from your customer relationships, and what you plan to give customers in return. All parts of the organization should coordinate in the execution of your CRM strategy — from marketing to contact center operations.

The execution of the CRM strategy includes three components: people, process, and technology. As with many contact center initiatives, it is very easy to purchase technology in the hopes that it will solve your problems and achieve your strategic goals. But careful advance planning and evaluation are necessary to ensure that the technology can actually improve your customer relationship management and your business results.

Using CRM data

Make data analysis part of your overall CRM strategy. This analysis can be as simple as preparing reports and conducting database queries, or as complex as building predictive models in an effort to forecast the future behavior of your customers.

In the contact center, the collected customer information is used to create business rules. Some rules guide agents in the handling of specific customer calls. For example, VIP customers can be identified by automatic number identification from their home phone, and their calls can be routed to your best agents. After the customer's call is answered, agents are prompted by the CRM tools to make specific offers that analysis suggests the customer may be interested in.

CRM applications are not unlike the contact center applications on the agents' workstation. They include ways to access customer information and deliver information to the customer. In a CRM environment they have additional functionality, such as information on the customer's call history and preferences, suggested sales and service strategies, and even suggested scripting.

Focusing on the customer

CRM applications can help a contact center totally shift their focus to the customer in ways never before possible. Contact center applications and infrastructure act as the enabler for CRM applications to really strut their stuff. If your infrastructure and applications cannot connect agents to the right information within the right time, the customers' experience and the entire operation is less effective.

However, if your CRM applications are meaningfully integrated within your infrastructure, then your customers' experience is enhanced and operations effectiveness is improved. Customers are properly identified, classified, and routed to the best available resource to help them. In addition, the agents receive the right information on their desktops to best address the customers' needs, as well as cross-sell and up-sell.

How to Recommend Technology

Okay, you're a technology genius and you found some technology that's going to make a big difference. So what's next?

How do you go about getting approval so you can start saving the company money? Why not keep it simple? Try the one-page cost-benefit analysis.

The one-page cost-benefit analysis

The most appropriate and effective way to submit a proposal for technology enhancements is with a one-page cost-benefit analysis. It's easy, and only two specific rules apply:

- ✔ The analysis must easily fit onto one letter-sized piece of paper
- ✔ The argument for spending money on new technology must be communicated in one minute or less

Certainly, some proposals are going to be a lot longer than one page. The point is that the business case for new technology needs to be so clear and so focused on business objectives and drivers that it can easily be summarized in one page. And you know what? Few decision makers ever read those other pages anyway.

The easiest way to meet both of these rules is to use the business model outlined in Part II. The model says that all business activities go toward the key objectives of generating revenue, minimizing cost, or satisfying customers. To make the case for new technology, you have to define the benefit of new technology in terms of those key business objectives.

To make your business case, you have to show that the new technology can affect at least one of the performance drivers in a manner that results in a benefit to your company substantially larger than the cost of that new technology.

Considering the technology payback

Any technology recommendation needs to take into consideration payback—after all, that is the reason that any cost-benefit analysis is done. The goal of the analysis is to show that the payback of any technology investment is greater than the investment.

When considering payback, however, you must also consider intangibles. For instance, if a new system can decrease average call length by 30 seconds, that's an easy savings to quantify. If the same system can also increase agent satisfaction, how do you quantify that? Further, how do you even determine that increased satisfaction is a potential payback until you've had agents try the new system?

These are questions that analysts face every day. As you are working on your recommendation, consider working with your existing analysts; they may be able to identify and quantify items that you never considered in your research. They definitely can help you identify current costs and measurements so you can compare them to the anticipated costs and measurements of the target system.

When considering any technology investment, work closely with your vendor or technology partners. Chances are good that they have experience in identifying and quantifying different ways that your investment can provide the payback you need.

Also consider payback in terms of strategic positioning — does a proposed system help position your contact center for greater growth or competitive advantage? Such intangibles are important in any business, and rightfully enter into any payback consideration for contact centers.

BUPA Australia improves customer care

BUPA Australia is the third largest health fund in Australia, and part of the worldwide British United Provident Association (BUPA). BUPA Australia looks after the healthcare needs of almost one million people across Australia and operates a contact center with 130 agents to service those customers.

When BUPA Australia decided to upgrade their contact center they wanted to ensure their customers would receive the highest level of care right from the first contact. The company chose an Avaya platform because they wanted a scalable platform that would support blended media and enable them to implement

IP technology across their branch network. "Avaya Australia's ability to provide a solution that allows us to mix traditional and IP Telephony, as well as giving a roadmap for multimedia contact management with short term ROI were important factors in our decision," said Julian Butler, Network System Manager, BUPA.

Serving up a solution

The new solution needed to provide for a large number of agents, system redundancy/disaster recovery options, reduced calling costs, and future flexibility. After extensive research, BUPA chose the Avaya S8700 Media Server, to support distributed IP networking and centralized call processing across multi-protocol networks, as well as Avaya Business Advocate skills-based call routing, Avaya Call Management System (CMS), and comprehensive reporting.

The solutions also had to integrate with BUPA's existing automated response system, which handled online payments. Working with an Avaya BusinessPartner, the implementation was effective and accurate the first time. "The idea was not to lose a second of contact. We wanted our customers to have no visibility of the work going on behind the scenes," said Butler. "We needed to

have people dial into our contact center and notice that service was enhanced; it was unacceptable for them to get dead air or a busy tone. And we achieved that."

Benefiting customers with improved service

Previously, when a caller dialed a branch they were connected to a system that had no ability to route to an available agent and no visibility for how the call was handled. "We can now route all customer calls, whether they dial a branch or whether they dial a contact center, so that they are delivered to the first available agent with the best matrix of skills," said Butler.

Saving costs today and positioning for tomorrow

The new contact center also improved BUPA's overall staff productivity, with the Avaya solution enabling reduced call times, call abandons, and callback for agents. The new solution will also result in BUPA saving on their call costs, allowing them to achieve a short term ROI.

The multimedia interoperability of the Avaya solutions also means that BUPA can gradually expand to other BUPA contact centers worldwide, creating a virtual contact center.

Part VI

Ten Ways to Improve Your Contact Center

● ●

In This Chapter

▶ Control your call characteristics

▶ Get a handle on call processes

▶ Make your contact center larger

▶ Mix types of work for better agent utilization

▶ Train during idle time

▶ Look for ways to offload unnecessary contacts

▶ Enhance customer support with speech

▶ Discover what it costs to take agents off the phones

▶ Invest in your staff

▶ Become a proactive manager

● ●

*G*enerally speaking, contact centers provide a very efficient way to communicate with a large number of customers. However, since contact center expenditures are frequently one of the larger line items for corporations, the costs are usually closely scrutinized.

In this part you find some general tips for improving your contact center by implementing efficiencies and decreasing overall costs.

Improve Call Control and Map Call Processes

Implementing a better call control strategy can have an immediate impact because reducing call length without sacrificing service is an effective way to reduce costs.

A good way to improve control is through the development of a contact guide. Guides can be as simple as an outline of the general flow and content of each contact — perhaps on one piece of paper — or can be very complex, using sophisticated scripting software and logical branching.

Any control mechanism you put in place for phone calls can also be generalized and adapted for other contact methods as well — including web, chat, e-mail, and self-service. The idea is to improve the customer experience by ensuring the contact never takes longer than is necessary to achieve a satisfactory resolution.

Mapping your processes for handling various types of customer calls is another useful exercise. Start by identifying the eight to ten primary reasons customers contact your center. Then, sit down with a group of agents, perhaps a supervisor or two, and a trainer to map out (on paper or in software) how each contact is to be handled.

After you map the top call types, you can ask the group the question, "How might this be done better?" Simplifying and improving processes can result in tremendous improvements to call length and other call objectives.

Enlarge Your Contact Center

You can enlarge your contact center in many ways — and not all of them involve using more physical space. In general, larger contact centers are more efficient than smaller centers.

The easiest way to make your contact center bigger is to work together. If your contact center is running separate call-handling groups (customer service and collections, for example), then by merging these two groups you can take advantage of the economies of bigger contact centers.

You can continue to have call-handling groups logically separated, but with the ability for available agents in one area to handle overflow in the other area.

Implementing an IP contact center can help make your operation more scalable, which means you can enlarge without costly build-outs or investments in your plant. Instead, you can utilize and manage agents — through your IP infrastructure — as if they were physically in your office.

You can also expand your contact center to take advantage of personnel in lower-cost labor markets. If your contact center is located in the heart of Capital City you may have access to lots of the best-qualified people, but they're likely to be expensive. It often doesn't cost as much for the same quality of staff in Rural City, USA; Frostbite Falls, Canada; or Farfaraway, India. If you have an IP contact center, expanding in such markets is much easier than in traditional contact centers.

Blend Work

You can benefit from improved agent occupancy by *blending* work into your contact-handling queue. A classic example of blending is mixing outbound telemarketing into an inbound sales or service queue. In this case, you make use of agent *idle time* — time agents spend waiting for incoming calls — to do your outbound work. As a result, your agents are busier (more occupied) overall. Should inbound volumes increase or spike, your agents stop making outbound calls while they handle the inbound calls.

Outbound collections calls and customer-service "welcome" calls can also be used for blending, perhaps as an alternative to telemarketing. Or, other types of work can be blended in, such as answering e-mail, chat, or regular mail.

Provide your agents with tools to maximize their efficiency. By providing screen pops of relevant information, an easy-to-use agent desktop, perhaps softphone, and the ability to access experts for the tough questions, you increase the number of one-call resolutions and customer satisfaction. And, you decrease the overall volume of calls to your contact center.

Turn Idle Time into Productive Training Time

Even in larger, more efficient contact centers, idle time can make up 15 percent or more of an agent's day. You can monitor agent activity and inbound call loads, and when agents have sufficient idle time, a CTI system can send training material to the agent's desktop. If the application is sophisticated enough, material can be customized to the needs of the individual agent, and testing can also be added.

Eliminate Unnecessary Calls

Unnecessary calls come from a variety of sources, including calls handled poorly on the first attempt, confusing marketing materials, incorrect or confusing invoices, misdirected calls, and so on. Reducing them is a basic step in increasing contact center efficiency. Here are three quick ways to reduce unnecessary calls:

✔ **Implement an IVR.** Using an integrated voice response — where automated voice prompts used to service customer contacts — offers customers a fast and efficient means of self-serving their calling needs 7 days a week, 24 hours a day. Depending on the environment, an IVR can offload between 5 and 25 percent or more of your center's call volume.

✔ **Use Web pages.** The use of company Web pages to provide customers with self-service options probably has a bright future. Self-service through a company Web site is cheaper than via an IVR, it's generally always available, and the complexity of transactions that can be done through the Internet is greater than any IVR solution.

✔ **Analyze why customers are calling.** A slightly more complex way to reduce unnecessary calls is to track the reasons for the contacts. Tracking, in detail, why customers call highlights the number of call types that are unnecessary and avoidable.

Add Speech Self-Service

Although speech self-service can reasonably be considered a method of eliminating unnecessary phone calls, the technology's promise to leverage existing Web investments really makes it stand out. In a speech self-service system, your "automated agents" can understand normal human speech and provide the information needed by customers. Beyond automated agent interactions, today's speech automated systems use open standards technologies like VoiceXML to better leverage existing Web self-service investments. This information can be provided quicker over any telephone and with less frustration than with a more traditional touchtone system. (Customers can get tired waiting for "press 1 for this, 2 for that, and 3 for something else.")

Find Out What a Change in Agent Utilization Costs

You can't chain your agents to their desks; they need time for breaks, meetings, training, and coaching. In most operations, you also find a certain amount of time that's unaccounted for. This missing time happens for a number of reasons and is probably acceptable so long as it doesn't get out of hand — no more than a few percent, for example.

Every percentage reduction in *agent utilization* — the percentage of time agents are actually logged in to the phone systems, compared to the total time they're being paid for — costs the contact center thousands of dollars per month. So, when you plan meetings, training, and so on, keep the cost-benefit in mind.

Spend More on Staff

Sooner or later, most contact centers fall into the trap of focusing too heavily on cost of labor. In fact, much of the outsourcing industry has been stuck in this dilemma.

It goes like this: Senior management wants the lowest possible cost of service. As a result, you reduce wages. You then spend more time than usual sifting through recruits trying to find the best cheap labor. You might even spend a lot of time training, but you don't want to overdo it because training is expensive. Once the agents are active you do your best to monitor, coach, and program them to make them the best that they can be.

What you end up with is cheaper labor with reduced skill and motivation. As a result, although the cost of your service is low, the capability is also low. Results of this cheaper service include longer calls, less revenue generation, the need for more training, substantially higher levels of errors and call-backs, and, ultimately, dissatisfied customers who may stop doing business with you.

Bottom line: Consider spending a bit more on labor up front.

Proactively Monitor and Manage

You meet two types of managers: reactive and proactive. Those in the former group are perpetually behind the gun, racing to get on top of some problem or catch up with the competition. Those in the latter group analyze data, anticipate problems, and plan for changes that head off the competition.

If you want to be proactive, learn what reporting capabilities your systems have and how you can best use the data they provide. If you're running an IP contact center, pay attention to reports generated not only in your contact center applications, but in your network management systems. Over time you can identify opportunities and circumvent potential problems, all to the benefit of your organization.

If your converged network is brand new, don't be afraid to seek outside help from qualified vendors — such as Avaya — to help you make sense of the new management tools you'll have available.

Upscaling UpSource to deliver cost-effective reliability

When you lose calls, you lose revenue — and ultimately your customers. But you can stop that cycle, as did UpSource, a company that delivers high-quality customer service and sales support for organizations of all sizes, leveraging outstanding agents and industry-leading technology to service customers quickly and efficiently. When UpSource experienced 13 major system failures over a one-year period, it was time to start looking at other solutions.

With their main office in Cambridge, Massachusetts, and a contact center in Nova Scotia, UpSource understands the benefits of establishing a cost-effective communications network designed to enhance productivity. It also understands the importance of using a single system that allows consistent applications to be used across the entire infrastructure. The network and software must be able to handle and route calls at a reasonable cost, allow agents to immediately retrieve caller information on their desktop terminals, and provide a high degree of reliability with no downtime.

Prior to the Avaya solution, Upsource had an existing system for call routing and distribution, Voice over IP (VoIP), and CRM. In its upgrade, UpSource was looking for reliability, sustainability, ease of use and management, and cost-effectiveness. The Upsource team chose to replace the existing infrastructure with an Avaya solution because they believed that Avaya had the strongest contact center platform and the broadest experience with convergence and IP Telephony.

UpSource concluded that Avaya also offered unparalleled reliability and cost-savings. The company expected the new solution to improve its competitive advantage through unique predictive routing capabilities, as well as protect its investment as it moves further into a converged networking environment. Cost was the final deciding factor. To grow the contact center by 500 percent (which UpSource expected to do), the Avaya solution cost significantly less than expanding the existing system.

An inside look at the Avaya solution

The Avaya solution is based on Avaya MultiVantage Communications Applications and Avaya Converged Infrastructure. It includes an Avaya DEFINITY Server SI powered by Avaya Communication Manager as well as Avaya Call Center Software for call routing, distribution, and reporting. The Avaya MultiVantage System offers a suite of call-routing capabilities that help agents handle calls more effectively. Among other leading features, it gives contact centers the flexibility of sending the appropriate calls to the appropriately skilled agent, within the center's business rules. Also included

(continued)

(continued)

are Avaya Computer Telephony and Avaya Contact Center Express, which offer intelligent screen pop at the agent desktop — in other words, the software takes information about an incoming call from Avaya Communication Manager, and then automatically opens a window on the agent's computer screen that has as much information about the caller and the question or problem as possible.

The bottom line for UpSource

Benefits of the Avaya solution go well beyond dollars and statistics. Reliability and stability top their list. The new system has been in place since December 2002, without a single outage. This is in part due to Avaya EXPERT Systems Diagnostic Tools, which work to identify and prevent problems before they arise, minimize their impact if they occur, and identify ways to keep them from taking place again.

Eliminating outages not only increases user productivity (and revenue), but is important for UpSource's credibility with its clients. Having a solid solution that does not go down means that UpSource's staff need not invest time in troubleshooting problems, and can instead focus on providing customer service and new client implementation.

Case Study

Racing to Contact Center Victory

● ●

*W*hen powerful NASCAR racers roar 'round the dramatically banked turns of Daytona International Speedway each February, race fans may be too excited to think about the behind-the-scenes companies that help fuel the remarkable growth of auto racing.

But one of those companies — International Speedway Corporation (ISC) — is thinking about the fans. A new Avaya customer contact center is speeding ticket sales, giving fans new sources of race information, and enabling ISC managers to integrate and manage customer service across all 12 ISC racetracks. Avaya's high-performance customer care solution is designed to steer ISC into first place with their fans by putting them on the fast track to service.

About International Speedway Corporation

Publicly-traded International Speedway Corporation is a leading promoter of motor sports activities in the United States. ISC owns and operates racetracks in Florida, Alabama, Arizona, South Carolina, and California, including some of the world's most famous racetracks (Talladega Superspeedway, Watkins Glen International, and Daytona International Speedway).

ISC racetracks host about 100 racing events throughout the year, including numerous events for NASCAR and other auto and motorcycle racing organizations. ISC generates revenue primarily from admissions, television, radio and ancillary rights fees, promotion and sponsorship fees, hospitality rentals, advertising revenues, and royalties.

A Challenge to Improve

Historically, ticket sales for ISC-hosted events were independently handled through telephone contacts at ticket offices at each of the twelve racetracks. With stand-alone ticket offices, however, ISC was missing out on opportunities to unify and streamline management and operations. Their past operations were essentially islands which could not enable agents from less-busy racetracks to back up other racetracks during peak fan demand. Statistics on call handling, such as customer wait times and average call handling time, were not uniformly collected or effectively managed. And ISC had no opportunity to integrate new technologies, such as the Internet and e-mail, for selling to and communicating with fans.

ISC managers decided to explore the benefits of creating a centralized contact center. The in-house expert was ISC contact center director Tom Canello. "We wanted to improve the level of service for our fans," Canello stated. "At each track, the staff operated a ticket office. They're selling tickets at the walk-up, they're fulfilling tickets, they're mailing — they're doing 10,000 other things. Taking ticket sales over the phone was just part of what they did. They weren't specifically trained to handle our race fans as efficiently and productively as a contact center agent could."

Implementing a Solution

After establishing a detailed set of specifications and going through a proposal process in early 2003, ISC selected Avaya to provide the contact center solution, with Avaya Global Services to provide long-term maintenance services. A factor in the decision, according to Canello, was the ability for Avaya to create a virtual contact center that included not just the actual contact center agents, but also ticket personnel at the individual racetracks. "With the Avaya solution, we knew we could equip all the racetrack sites with the IP Agent application," Canello says.

The deadline to install the Avaya contact center solution for Phase One — including Avaya DEFINITY G3si Communications Server and an Avaya SCC1 Media Gateway running Avaya

Communication Manager, Avaya Call Management System, Avaya Interactive Response and Avaya INTUITY AUDIX voice messaging—was a short five months. An important part of the installation was Computer Telephony Integration (CTI) capabilities, made possible via the Avaya Interaction Center application.

Realizing Quantifiable Benefits

After only months of operation, the rich flow of information from his new Avaya contact center is giving Canello invaluable new insight into how ISC is really serving its fans, and helping boost sales. Employees working in ticket offices at distant racetracks supplement a central contact center in Daytona Beach, staffed by 50 to 70 agents depending on the season. All are connected through a single integrated Avaya automatic call distributor and CTI system.

"With centralized contact center reporting across all locations, it's just amazing what you can learn about the business—how to improve a revenue stream, how to run the business more efficiently," Canello observes. ISC has realized major gains in customer service and support, agent productivity, and knowledge throughout the company.

Customer service and support

To increase responsiveness to thousands of information requests without taking valuable agent time, ISC deployed Avaya Interactive Response. Based on the caller's request, Avaya Interaction Center connects the fan to an agent or to a set of Frequently Asked Questions (FAQ) on Interactive Response that help fans get answers on the track in question.

ISC estimates that Avaya Interactive Response is accessed by approximately 8 to 10 percent of incoming calls. This feature helps ISC to grow productively by handling more callers without increasing staff. Even more important for fans is the increased accessibility to timely racetrack information.

"Giving fans the option to hear recorded information frees our agents to help others who really need personal attention, and to focus on high-value ticket sales," says Canello. "Of course, if an FAQ caller decides that they want to talk to an agent, our Avaya solution makes the transfer seamless and easy."

Agent productivity

In the past, only 23 percent of calls to ISC racetracks resulted in ticket sales. That's because the agents were spending a lot of time answering questions from fans — answers that Avaya Interactive Response now provides. "We have seen a jump in our call-to-order ratio, there's no doubt about that," says Canello.

By matching Automatic Number Identification (ANI) information with customer records, Avaya Interaction Center instantly gives agents valuable customer information via a "screen pop," an advantage Canello estimates can shave 30 to 40 seconds off the average time for each call. The reduction in call handling time provides an immediate 8 percent productivity gain.

Increased knowledge

"Our ticket offices are great ticket-selling people, but now they're starting to understand what the value of having a call center is all about," says Canello. "Average talk time, average speed of answer, IVR automation rates, after-call work — it's educating the people in the ticket offices to better understand how we can better serve the fans, and how productive we are." The result is a win both for ISC, which is operating more productively, and for fans, who still have access to on-site knowledge from employees at the local racetrack ticket offices.

To ensure the consistent delivery of high quality service to the customers, the contact center has added a NICE Quality monitoring system to systematically record customer interactions with agents based on a variety of criteria. These interactions enable supervisors to coach agents more effectively and determine the need for supplemental training. And now, by serving its customers more effectively with the Avaya Customer Interaction Suite, ISC has added a critical ingredient to its formula for victory.